Trucks and Earthmovers

by Gabby Goldsack

WATERBIRD BOOKS

Columbus, Ohio

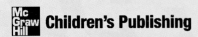 **Children's Publishing**

This edition published in the United States of America in 2004 by
Waterbird Books
an imprint of McGraw-Hill Children's Publishing,
a Division of The McGraw-Hill Companies
8787 Orion Place
Columbus, Ohio 43240-4027

www.MHkids.com

Library of Congress Cataloging-in-Publication Data is on file with the publisher.

First published in Great Britain in 2004 by ticktock Media Ltd.,
Unit 2, Orchard Business Centre, North Farm Road, Tunbridge Wells, Kent TN3 3XF.
Text and illustrations © 2004 ticktock Entertainment Ltd.
We would like to thank: Meme Ltd.
Picture Credits: Mack Trucks 4, 5. Peterbuilt Trucks 4, 5, 14, 22, 27. Saab Scania 8. New Holland Ltd.10–13.
Every effort has been made to trace the copyright holders, and we apologize in advance for any unintentional omissions.
We would be pleased to insert the appropriate acknowledgements in any subsequent edition of this publication.

All rights reserved. Except as permitted under the United States Copyright Act, no part of this publication may be reproduced or
distributed in any form or by any means, or stored in a database retrieval system, without prior written permission from the publisher.

Printed in China

1-57768-901-1

1 2 3 4 5 6 7 8 9 10 TTM 09 08 07 06 05 04
The **McGraw·Hill** Companies

Contents

Note to Parents and Teachers

The Busy Books series is designed to be both stimulating and accessible to young readers. Studies show that young children learn well through sharing. The activities in this book have been created with just that in mind. They provide an opportunity for you and your child to talk about the activities on each page. Stories, games, comprehension questions, and counting exercises offer a variety of ways to help your child learn new words, build basic skills, and practice letter and number recognition. Encourage your child to ask questions as you read together. By working with your child, you will be preparing him or her for the learning years ahead.

Trucks and Earthmovers:
Trucks at Work

There are many different types of trucks.
Some trucks help people who are building roads.
Others carry food or gasoline. There are even trucks
that carry other trucks.

This **garbage truck**
picks up trash and
then takes it to the
dump to help keep
our cities clean.

The **heavy
loader** truck is
powerful, but it
cannot go very
fast with a huge
load on board.

cab

4

grill

This truck is called a cement mixer. The truck stores cement and mixes it as it drives along. The whole back spins around slowly.

The back of the **dump truck** lifts up to let the load slide out.

lights

Truck Words

Can you find these words on the page?

lights

garbage truck

heavy loader

cab

dump truck

cement mixer

grill

Trucks and Earthmovers:
Earthmovers at Work

Earthmovers work on construction sites.

An earthmover can lift and push earth around by using its arm and bucket. Some earthmovers have wheels and some have tracks.

bucket

This **earthmover** has bigger wheels than any car. It carries big piles of dirt in its enormous bucket.

The tracks on this **bulldozer** help it grip as it pushes huge piles of dirt.

tracks

arms

This **digger** has two arms. The bucket on the back digs holes, while the shovel on the front scoops and lifts dirt.

tire

This **dump truck** is so big that it is not allowed to travel on some roads. Trucks like these are used to move enormous loads of rock, dirt, or coal.

Earthmover Words

Can you find these words on the page?

bucket

earthmover

bulldozer

dump truck

tracks

digger

arms

Word Puzzles

Look at these truck and earthmover pictures.

Can you tell what order the words should go in?

1

TransWest
SCANIA
124G 470

truck

big

The

red

is

Truck and Earthmover Words

You have seen these words before. Use the pictures to help you say them.

tire

grill

MACK

2

can

digger

I

the

see

cold

snow

The

is

3

bucket

light

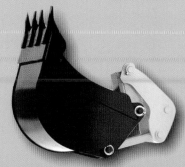

cab

Word Puzzles answers: **1.** The big truck is red. **2.** I can see the digger. **3.** The snow is cold.

A Story to Read:
The Very Useful Tractor

This is **Bill the farmer**.

His tractor is bright **blue**.

The engine rumbles loudly
as the tractor plows the field.

Farmer Bill is in his tractor. He sees his farmer friend and gives him a wave.

Farmer Bill's tractor is always moving. Look at it go!

This tractor can do many jobs. It pushes dirt and plows fields.

This giant combine harvester is cutting the **grain**. The farmer wants to cut the grain before it rains.

The grain is tipped into the trailer. It is a heavy load! The tractor tows the trailer along the winding road.

Next, the tractor gathers **hay**. The hay is saved for the animals to eat in colder weather.

It is getting dark! Time to park the tractor in the shed.

Can you answer these questions about the story you have just read?

1 Who is driving the tractor?
2 What color is the tractor?
3 What does the combine harvester cut?

A Story to Share:
Carl's Busy Day

Say the **boldface** words out loud.

Carl drives a car transporter that delivers **cars** to people. Carl thinks that delivering cars is fun, but he wonders what it would be like to have another job.

Carl's first stop is the shipyard. *Creeeeeak!* goes the crane as it lifts a car onto the ship. *Driving a crane could be fun,* thinks Carl.

Carl's next stop is the quarry. *Honk! Honk!* toots the horn of a **low loader** as it drives past. It is carrying a load of heavy rocks.

Driving a low loader could be fun, thinks Carl.

At the quarry, Carl unloads a new car for the supervisor. Nearby, a **dump truck** unloads a mountain of dirt.

Driving a dump truck could be fun, thinks Carl.

Next, there are new cars to deliver to the garage. *Wow*, thinks Carl when he sees a **gasoline tanker**. The license plate on the tanker shows that the driver has come a long way. *Driving a gasoline tanker could be fun*, thinks Carl.

Carl sees a **semitrailer** fly past. *Tooooooooot!* goes the truck. The driver of the truck is in a hurry because he needs to deliver supplies to a store. *Driving a semitrailer could be fun,* thinks Carl.

Next, Carl delivers a car to the construction site. A **cement mixer** is there. The body of the mixer is always turning so that the cement does not harden. *Driving a cement mixer could be fun,* thinks Carl. Everyone stops working to look at the new car that Carl delivered. All of the workers tell Carl that he is lucky because he gets to deliver new cars to people.

Back at the car depot, Carl loads his transporter with more cars. It looks like another busy day tomorrow. But Carl is happy with his job. *Driving a car transporter is fun,* Carl thinks.

Building a Road
Game

Different trucks and earthmovers are needed to build a road. Who will finish first?

This fun road game is for 2 to 4 players.

First, find a small plastic toy for each player. Place each toy on the start line. Then, roll a die to see who goes first. The player who rolls the highest number goes first. Take turns moving along the road, counting as you go. Follow the instructions on the signs that you land on. The first person to finish building the road wins!

START

9

10

Dump load in the wrong spot. Lose a turn!

FINISH

Hooray! The road is finished. You win!

19

1
2
3
Stop to unload a truck. Lose a turn!
4
8
7
Cement truck is late. Go back 3 spaces.
6
5
Fill up dumper. Take an extra turn!
MACK
11
12
Finish painting lines on road. Go forward three spaces.
13
14
18
17
16
Use digger to speed up job. Take an extra turn!
15

A Bedtime Story:
Tommy's Party

Tommy couldn't wait for his birthday to arrive. He was going to have a truck party! His mom offered to make a birthday cake that looked just like a truck. It would be covered with red and yellow icing, and it would have chocolate cookies for wheels, jellybeans for lights, licorice strips for the grill, and a trailer full of candy.

But best of all, Tommy's dad was a truck driver, and he had agreed to let all Tommy's friends have a ride in his big, red truck!

When the big day arrived, it was raining hard. Tommy's dad came into Tommy's bedroom very early to say happy birthday. He had to go to the construction site to make a delivery but promised to be home in plenty of time for the party.

Tommy had a very busy morning helping his mom make the truck cake (and licking the bowl and spoon) and collecting his birthday mail. Pretty soon, his friends arrived. Tommy got lots of truck presents from his friends. Julie gave him a book filled with pictures of trucks, and Bruce gave him a toy truck. Tommy thanked his friends and told them that, as a special treat, his dad would let them all have rides in his truck. But wait a minute. Where was Tommy's dad?

At the construction site, Tommy's dad had a problem. It had been raining hard all morning, and the construction site was covered in deep, sticky mud. The truck was stuck! Tommy's dad had been trying to get the truck out of the mud. He gritted his teeth, gripped the steering wheel, and put his foot down hard on the gas pedal. The engine let out a loud, *vroooooooooom!*, but still no luck. The big, red truck was stuck!

What was he going to do? Tommy was counting on him to bring his truck to the party. Just then, out of the corner of his eye, Tommy's dad saw something. The bulldozer on the construction site had also gotten stuck in the mud, and a huge tow truck had just arrived to tow it out. Quickly, Tommy's dad jumped out of the cab of his truck and ran over to where the tow truck had pulled up.

Tommy's dad waved his arms at the driver. "Please, before you tow the bulldozer, can you tow my truck out of the mud? I promised my son that I would come to his birthday party!" he shouted.

"It would be my pleasure," said the driver. He drove the tow truck over to where Tommy's dad's truck was stuck.

The tow truck driver attached a steel cord to the front of Tommy's dad's truck. "Now, get behind the wheel of your truck. On the count of three, get ready to steer," said the driver as he revved his powerful engine. Tommy's dad did as he was told. "Ready? Okay. 1…2…3!" called the tow-truck driver.

Back at home, Tommy was just about to tell his friends that the truck rides weren't going to happen after all when, from outside, there came the sound of a truck's deep *tooooooooot!* Tommy's friends rushed to the window to see. And there, coming up the street, was Tommy's dad's truck. Tommy's friends all cheered.

"Now we can have rides in Dad's big, red truck!" said Tommy proudly. And they did. Afterward, they each ate a big piece of Mom's truck cake.

Truck Counting: How Many Earthmovers?

How many earthmovers are there in each line?

Can you count them?

Which line has the most earthmovers in it? Which line has the least?

Number words

One

Two

Three

Four

Five

Six

Can you match the number words to the right group of vehicles?
Use the color codes to help you.

Truck Counting:
Load the Trucks

Can you help to load the trucks?

Look at these two trucks. They look the same, but they have different loads. Which one will be quicker to load?

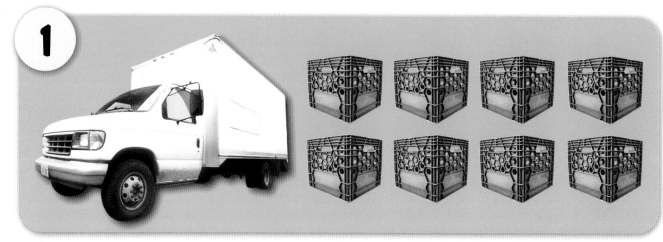

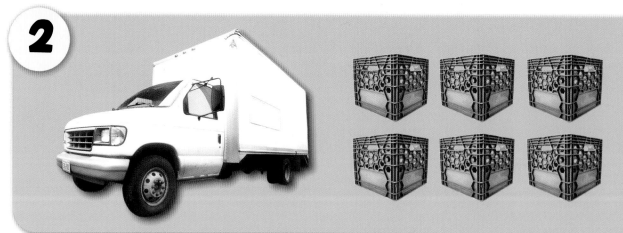

How many crates does truck 1 have to load?

How many crates does truck 2 have to load?

Can you match each load to the right truck?

Use the color clues to help you.

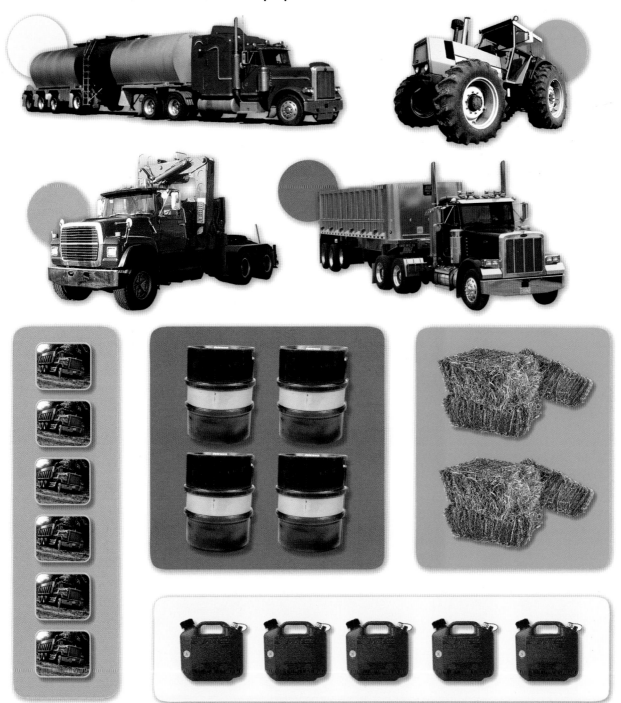

Which truck do you think will finish loading first?

Which truck has six things to load?

Spot the Difference

Truck and earthmover drivers need to be alert when using their vehicles. They need to be able to know when something is wrong.

Look at these two pictures.
Can you spot the four differences between them?

Answers: 1. The digger has changed from yellow to red. **2.** The arm on the back of the digger is missing. **3.** The load from the dump truck is missing. **4.** The back of the dump truck has changed from yellow to green.

Make a Digger

Follow these instructions to make your own digger.
You will need an adult to help you.

You will need: **1.** a big shoe box **2.** tubes from two paper towel rolls **3.** a smaller box (without a lid) **4.** plastic bottle tops **5.** glue and scissors **6.** paints and paintbrush

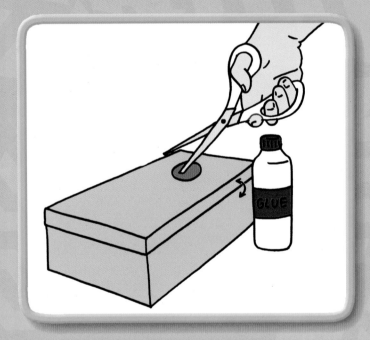

1. Draw a circle at one end of the lid of the shoe box by tracing around the end of the paper towel tube. Ask an adult to cut out the hole as shown. Then, glue the lid onto the shoe box.

2. Next, ask the adult to make a hole at the end of one of the tubes as shown.

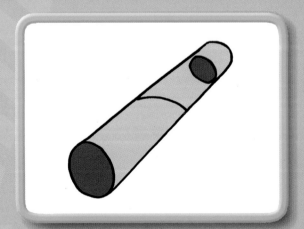

3. Push the second tube through the hole in the first tube to make an L shape. Use glue to hold the tubes together if needed. (You may need an adult to help you.)

4. Glue the inside of the smaller box to the end of the second tube as shown. Push the digger's L-shaped arm through the hole in the shoe box lid as shown. The L-shaped arm should lean on an angle.

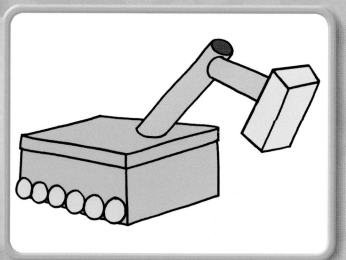

5. Glue the plastic bottle tops on each side of the shoe box to make the wheels. Now, you can paint your digger. Look at the pictures in this book to see which colors to use.

You should be able to put small loads into the scoop of your digger. What happens if you put some gravel into the scoop?

Word Finder

Here are some of the words used in this book. Can you remember what they mean? Go back and look through the book to see if you can find each word again.

truck · gasoline · dirt

earthmover · tractor · tire

grill · tracks · grain

digger · bulldozer · hay

red · cement · farmer

arms · bucket · blue

lights · plow · cab